CHINESE
HOROSCOPES
FOR
LOVERS

The
Dragon

LORI REID

illustrated by
PAUL COLLICUTT

❖

ELEMENT BOOKS

Shaftesbury, Dorset • Rockport, Massachusetts • Brisbane, Queensland

© Lori Reid 1996

First published in Great Britain in 1996 by

ELEMENT BOOKS LIMITED

Shaftesbury, Dorset SP7 8BP

Published in the USA in 1996 by

ELEMENT BOOKS, INC.

PO Box 830, Rockport, MA 01966

Published in Australia in 1996 by

ELEMENT BOOKS LIMITED

for JACARANDA WILEY LIMITED

33 Park Road, Milton, Brisbane 4064

Designed and created by

THE BRIDGEWATER BOOK COMPANY

Art directed by *Peter Bridgewater*

Designed by *Angela Neal*

Picture research by *Vanessa Fletcher*

Edited by *Gillian Delaforce*

Printed and bound in Great Britain by
BPC Paulton Books Ltd

British Library Cataloguing in Publication data available

Library of Congress Cataloging in Publication data available

ISBN 1-85230-765-X

Contents

8

*Why are
some people
lucky in
love and
others not?*

Chinese Astrology

SOME PEOPLE fall in love and, as the fairy tales go, live happily ever after. Others fall in love – again and again, make the same mistakes every time and never form a lasting relationship. Most of us come between these two extremes, and

some people form remarkably successful unions while others make spectacular disasters of their personal lives. Why are some people lucky in love while others have the odds stacked against them?

ANIMAL NAMES
According to the philosophy of the Far East, luck has very little to do with it. The answer, the philosophers say, lies with 'the Animal that hides in our hearts'. This Animal, of which there are 12, forms part of the complex art of Chinese Astrology. Each year of a 12-year cycle is attributed an Animal sign, whose characteristics are said to influence worldly events as well as the personality and fate of each living thing that comes under its dominion. The 12 Animals run in sequence, beginning with the Rat and followed by the Ox, Tiger, Rabbit, Dragon, Snake, Horse, Sheep, Monkey, Rooster, Dog and last, but not least, the Pig. Being born in the Year of the Ox, for example, is simply a way of describing what you're like, physically and psychologically. And this is quite different from someone who, for instance, is born in the Year of the Snake.

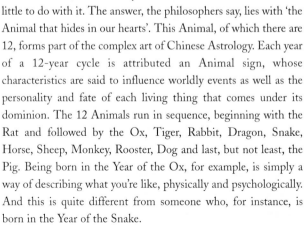

龍

9

The 12
Animals
of Chinese
Astrology.

RELATIONSHIPS

These Animal names are merely the tip of the
iceberg, considering the complexity of the whole subject. Yet such
are the richness and wisdom of Chinese Astrology that
understanding the principles behind the year in which you were
born will give you powerful insights into your own personality.
The system is very specific about which Animals are compatible
and which are antagonistic and this tells us whether our
relationships will be successful. Marriages are made in heaven, so
the saying goes. The heavens, according to Chinese beliefs, can
point the way. The rest is up to us.

10

The Western calendar is based on the Sun; the Oriental on the Moon.

Year Chart and Birth Dates

UNLIKE THE WESTERN CALENDAR, which is based on the Sun, the Oriental year is based on the movement of the Moon, which means that New Year's Day does not fall on a fixed date. This Year Chart, taken from the Chinese Perpetual Calendar, lists the dates on which each year begins and ends together with its Animal ruler for the year. In addition, the Chinese believe that the tangible world is composed of 5 elements, each slightly adapting the characteristics of the Animal signs. These elemental influences are also given here. Finally, the aspect, that is, whether the year is characteristically Yin (-) or Yang (+), is also listed.

YIN AND YANG

Yin and Yang are the terms given to the dynamic complementary forces that keep the universe in balance and which are the central principles behind life. Yin is all that is considered negative, passive, feminine, night, the Moon, while Yang is considered positive, active, masculine, day, the Sun.

11

Year	From – To	Animal sign	Element	Aspect	
1900	31 Jan 1900 – 18 Feb 1901	Rat	Metal	+	Yang
1901	19 Feb 1901 – 7 Feb 1902	Ox	Metal	–	Yin
1902	8 Feb 1902 – 28 Jan 1903	Tiger	Water	+	Yang
1903	29 Jan 1903 – 15 Feb 1904	Rabbit	Water	–	Yin
1904	16 Feb 1904 – 3 Feb 1905	Dragon	Wood	+	Yang
1905	4 Feb 1905 – 24 Jan 1906	Snake	Wood	–	Yin
1906	25 Jan 1906 – 12 Feb 1907	Horse	Fire	+	Yang
1907	13 Feb 1907 – 1 Feb 1908	Sheep	Fire	–	Yin
1908	2 Feb 1908 – 21 Jan 1909	Monkey	Earth	+	Yang
1909	22 Jan 1909 – 9 Feb 1910	Rooster	Earth	–	Yin
1910	10 Feb 1910 – 29 Jan 1911	Dog	Metal	+	Yang
1911	30 Jan 1911 – 17 Feb 1912	Pig	Metal	–	Yin
1912	18 Feb 1912 – 5 Feb 1913	Rat	Water	+	Yang
1913	6 Feb 1913 – 25 Jan 1914	Ox	Water	–	Yin
1914	26 Jan 1914 – 13 Feb 1915	Tiger	Wood	+	Yang
1915	14 Feb 1915 – 2 Feb 1916	Rabbit	Wood	–	Yin
1916	3 Feb 1916 – 22 Jan 1917	Dragon	Fire	+	Yang
1917	23 Jan 1917 – 10 Feb 1918	Snake	Fire	–	Yin
1918	11 Feb 1918 – 31 Jan 1919	Horse	Earth	+	Yang
1919	1 Feb 1919 – 19 Feb 1920	Sheep	Earth	–	Yin
1920	20 Feb 1920 – 7 Feb 1921	Monkey	Metal	+	Yang
1921	8 Feb 1921 – 27 Jan 1922	Rooster	Metal	–	Yin
1922	28 Jan 1922 – 15 Feb 1923	Dog	Water	+	Yang
1923	16 Feb 1923 – 4 Feb 1924	Pig	Water	–	Yin
1924	5 Feb 1924 – 24 Jan 1925	Rat	Wood	+	Yang
1925	25 Jan 1925 – 12 Feb 1926	Ox	Wood	–	Yin
1926	13 Feb 1926 – 1 Feb 1927	Tiger	Fire	+	Yang
1927	2 Feb 1927 – 22 Jan 1928	Rabbit	Fire	–	Yin
1928	23 Jan 1928 – 9 Feb 1929	Dragon	Earth	+	Yang
1929	10 Feb 1929 – 29 Jan 1930	Snake	Earth	–	Yin
1930	30 Jan 1930 – 16 Feb 1931	Horse	Metal	+	Yang
1931	17 Feb 1931 – 5 Feb 1932	Sheep	Metal	–	Yin
1932	6 Feb 1932 – 25 Jan 1933	Monkey	Water	+	Yang
1933	26 Jan 1933 – 13 Feb 1934	Rooster	Water	–	Yin
1934	14 Feb 1934 – 3 Feb 1935	Dog	Wood	+	Yang
1935	4 Feb 1935 – 23 Jan 1936	Pig	Wood	–	Yin

THE
DRAGON

龍

12

Year	From – To	Animal sign	Element	Aspect	
1936	24 Jan 1936 – 10 Feb 1937	Rat	Fire	+	Yang
1937	11 Feb 1937 – 30 Jan 1938	Ox	Fire	–	Yin
1938	31 Jan 1938 – 18 Feb 1939	Tiger	Earth	+	Yang
1939	19 Feb 1939 – 7 Feb 1940	Rabbit	Earth	–	Yin
1940	8 Feb 1940 – 26 Jan 1941	Dragon	Metal	+	Yang
1941	27 Jan 1941 – 14 Feb 1942	Snake	Metal	–	Yin
1942	15 Feb 1942 – 4 Feb 1943	Horse	Water	+	Yang
1943	5 Feb 1943 – 24 Jan 1944	Sheep	Water	–	Yin
1944	25 Jan 1944 – 12 Feb 1945	Monkey	Wood	+	Yang
1945	13 Feb 1945 – 1 Feb 1946	Rooster	Wood	–	Yin
1946	2 Feb 1946 – 21 Jan 1947	Dog	Fire	+	Yang
1947	22 Jan 1947 – 9 Feb 1948	Pig	Fire	–	Yin
1948	10 Feb 1948 – 28 Jan 1949	Rat	Earth	+	Yang
1949	29 Jan 1949 – 16 Feb 1950	Ox	Earth	–	Yin
1950	17 Feb 1950 –5 Feb 1951	Tiger	Metal	+	Yang
1951	6 Feb 1951 – 26 Jan 1952	Rabbit	Metal	–	Yin
1952	27 Jan 1952 – 13 Feb 1953	Dragon	Water	+	Yang
1953	14 Feb 1953 – 2 Feb 1954	Snake	Water	–	Yin
1954	3 Feb 1954 – 23 Jan 1955	Horse	Wood	+	Yang
1955	24 Jan 1955 – 11 Feb 1956	Sheep	Wood	–	Yin
1956	12 Feb 1956 – 30 Jan 1957	Monkey	Fire	+	Yang
1957	31 Jan 1957 – 17 Feb 1958	Rooster	Fire	–	Yin
1958	18 Feb 1958 – 7 Feb 1959	Dog	Earth	+	Yang
1959	8 Feb 1959 – 27 Jan 1960	Pig	Earth	–	Yin
1960	28 Jan 1960 – 14 Feb 1961	Rat	Metal	+	Yang
1961	15 Feb 1961 – 4 Feb 1962	Ox	Metal	–	Yin
1962	5 Feb 1962 – 24 Jan 1963	Tiger	Water	+	Yang
1963	25 Jan 1963 – 12 Feb 1964	Rabbit	Water	–	Yin
1964	13 Feb 1964 – 1 Feb 1965	Dragon	Wood	+	Yang
1965	2 Feb 1965 – 20 Jan 1966	Snake	Wood	–	Yin
1966	21 Jan 1966 – 8 Feb 1967	Horse	Fire	+	Yang
1967	9 Feb 1967 – 29 Jan 1968	Sheep	Fire	–	Yin
1968	30 Jan 1968 – 16 Feb 1969	Monkey	Earth	+	Yang
1969	17 Feb 1969 – 5 Feb 1970	Rooster	Earth	–	Yin
1970	6 Feb 1970 – 26 Jan 1971	Dog	Metal	+	Yang
1971	27 Jan 1971 – 15 Jan 1972	Pig	Metal	–	Yin

Year	From – To	Animal sign	Element	Aspect	
1972	16 Jan 1972 – 2 Feb 1973	Rat	Water	+	Yang
1973	3 Feb 1973 – 22 Jan 1974	Ox	Water	–	Yin
1974	23 Jan 1974 – 10 Feb 1975	Tiger	Wood	+	Yang
1975	11 Feb 1975 – 30 Jan 1976	Rabbit	Wood	–	Yin
1976	31 Jan 1976 – 17 Feb 1977	Dragon	Fire	+	Yang
1977	18 Feb 1977 – 6 Feb 1978	Snake	Fire	–	Yin
1978	7 Feb 1978 – 27 Jan 1979	Horse	Earth	+	Yang
1979	28 Jan 1979 – 15 Feb 1980	Sheep	Earth	–	Yin
1980	16 Feb 1980 – 4 Feb 1981	Monkey	Metal	+	Yang
1981	5 Feb 1981 – 24 Jan 1982	Rooster	Metal	–	Yin
1982	25 Jan 1982 – 12 Feb 1983	Dog	Water	+	Yang
1983	13 Feb 1983 – 1 Feb 1984	Pig	Water	–	Yin
1984	2 Feb 1984 – 19 Feb 1985	Rat	Wood	+	Yang
1985	20 Feb 1985 – 8 Feb 1986	Ox	Wood	–	Yin
1986	9 Feb 1986 – 28 Jan 1987	Tiger	Fire	+	Yang
1987	29 Jan 1987 – 16 Feb 1988	Rabbit	Fire	–	Yin
1988	17 Feb 1988 – 5 Feb 1989	Dragon	Earth	+	Yang
1989	6 Feb 1989 – 26 Jan 1990	Snake	Earth	–	Yin
1990	27 Jan 1990 – 14 Feb 1991	Horse	Metal	+	Yang
1991	15 Feb 1991 – 3 Feb 1992	Sheep	Metal	–	Yin
1992	4 Feb 1992 – 22 Jan 1993	Monkey	Water	+	Yang
1993	23 Jan 1993 – 9 Feb 1994	Rooster	Water	–	Yin
1994	10 Feb 1994 – 30 Jan 1995	Dog	Wood	+	Yang
1995	31 Jan 1995 – 18 Feb 1996	Pig	Wood	–	Yin
1996	19 Feb 1996 – 7 Feb 1997	Rat	Fire	+	Yang
1997	8 Feb 1997 – 27 Jan 1998	Ox	Fire	–	Yin
1998	28 Jan 1998 – 15 Feb 1999	Tiger	Earth	+	Yang
1999	16 Feb 1999 – 4 Feb 2000	Rabbit	Earth	–	Yin
2000	5 Feb 2000 – 23 Jan 2001	Dragon	Metal	+	Yang
2001	24 Jan 2001 – 11 Feb 2002	Snake	Metal	–	Yin
2002	12 Feb 2002 – 31 Jan 2003	Horse	Water	+	Yang
2003	1 Feb 2003 – 21 Jan 2004	Sheep	Water	–	Yin
2004	22 Jan 2004 – 8 Feb 2005	Monkey	Wood	+	Yang
2005	9 Feb 2005 – 28 Jan 2006	Rooster	Wood	–	Yin
2006	29 Jan 2006 – 17 Feb 2007	Dog	Fire	+	Yang
2007	18 Feb 2007 – 6 Feb 2008	Pig	Fire	–	Yin

13

14

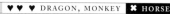

Introducing the Animals

| THE RAT | ♥ ♥ ♥ DRAGON, MONKEY | ✖ HORSE |

Outwardly cool, Rats are passionate lovers with depths of feeling that others don't often recognize. Rats are very self-controlled.

| THE OX | ♥ ♥ ♥ SNAKE, ROOSTER | ✖ SHEEP |

Not necessarily the most romantic of the signs, Ox people make steadfast lovers as well as faithful, affectionate partners.

| THE TIGER | ♥ ♥ ♥ HORSE, DOG | ✖ MONKEY |

Passionate and sensual, Tigers are exciting lovers. Flirty when young, once committed they make stable partners and keep their sexual allure.

| THE RABBIT | ♥ ♥ ♥ SHEEP, PIG | ✖ ROOSTER |

Gentle, emotional and sentimental, Rabbits make sensitive lovers. They are shrewd and seek a partner who offers security.

| THE DRAGON | ♥ ♥ ♥ RAT, MONKEY | ✖ DOG |

Dragon folk get as much stimulation from mind-touch as they do through sex. A partner on the same wave-length is essential.

| THE SNAKE | ♥ ♥ ♥ OX, ROOSTER | ✖ PIG |

Deeply passionate, strongly sexed but not aggressive, snakes are attracted to elegant, refined partners. But they are deeply jealous and possessive.

♥ ♥ ♥ COMPATIBLE   ✖ INCOMPATIBLE

15

THE HORSE	♥ ♥ ♥ TIGER, DOG	✖ RAT

 For horse-born folk love is blind. In losing their hearts, they lose their heads and make several mistakes before finding the right partner.

THE SHEEP	♥ ♥ ♥ RABBIT, PIG	✖ OX

 Sheep-born people are made for marriage. Domesticated home-lovers, they find emotional satisfaction with a partner who provides security.

THE MONKEY	♥ ♥ ♥ DRAGON, RAT	✖ TIGER

 Clever and witty, Monkeys need partners who will keep them stimulated. Forget the 9 to 5 routine, these people need *pizzazz*.

THE ROOSTER	♥ ♥ ♥ OX, SNAKE	✖ RABBIT

 The Rooster's stylish good looks guarantee they will attract many suitors. They are level-headed and approach relationships coolly.

THE DOG	♥ ♥ ♥ TIGER, HORSE	✖ DRAGON

 A loving, stable relationship is an essential component in the lives of Dogs. Once they have found their mate, they remain faithful for life.

THE PIG	♥ ♥ ♥ RABBIT, SHEEP	✖ SNAKE

 These are sensual hedonists who enjoy lingering love-making between satin sheets. Caviar and champagne go down very nicely too.

The Dragon Personality

YEARS OF THE DRAGON

1904 ★ 1916 ★ 1928 ★ 1940 ★ 1952

1964 ★ 1976 ★ 1988 ★ 2000

THE DRAGON IS A FABULOUS creature of myth and legend. Colourful, exotic, symbol of good fortune and emblem of power, the Oriental Dragon is regarded as a sacred beast, quite the reverse of the archetypal malevolent monster that Westerners feel compelled to defeat and slay. In Eastern philosophy, the Dragon is a bringer of luck and people born in Dragon Years are honoured and respected.

DRAGON FACTS

Fifth in order ★ *Chinese name – LONG* ★ *Sign of luck*
★ *Hour – 7AM–8.59AM* ★ *Month – April* ★
★ *Western counterpart – Aries* ★

CHARACTERISTICS

♥ *Originality* ♥ *Self-assurance* ♥ *Resourcefulness* ♥ *Adaptability*
♥ *Valour* ♥ *Enthusiasm*

✖ *Arrogance* ✖ *Tactlessness* ✖ *Hot-headedness* ✖ *Criticism*
✖ *Unpredictability* ✖ *Quick-temper*

龍

17

*Dragons
need to be
as free as
the clouds.*

FREE SPIRITS

Dragon folk are laws unto themselves. Being born into this sign means you're the free spirit of the Zodiac; having to conform is anathema to you. Rules and regulations are made for other people, not for you. Restrictions squeeze stone dead the creative germ that at every turn wants to spark into life. You need to be as free as the wind and the clouds which are your domain.

DRAGON PAGEANTRY

You're a gorgeous creature, as colourful and flamboyant as a gilded dragon in a Chinese pageant. A dynamo of energy, a supreme extrovert, gifted, original, exciting and utterly irrepressible, everything you do is on the grand scale – big ideas, extravagant gestures, massive ambitions. And because you're confident, enthusiastic and fearless in the face of challenge, you invariably succeed. Dragons, one way or another, usually make it to the top.

Bathing in the Ganges (detail)
PRINSEP VALENTINE CAMERON 1838–1904

Your Hour of Birth

WHILE YOUR YEAR OF BIRTH describes your fundamental character, the Animal governing the actual hour in which you were born describes your outer temperament, how people see you or the picture you present to the outside world. Note that each Animal rules over two consecutive hours. Also note that these are GMT standard times and that adjustments need to be made if you were born during Summer or daylight saving time.

11PM – 12.59AM ★ RAT

 Pleasant, sociable, easy to get on with. An active, confident, busy person – and a bit of a busybody to boot.

1AM – 2.59AM ★ OX

 Level-headed and down-to-earth, you come across as knowledgeable and reliable – sometimes, though, a bit biased.

3AM – 4.59AM ★ TIGER

 Enthusiastic and self-assured, people see you as a strong and positive personality – at times a little over-exuberant.

5AM – 6.59AM ★ RABBIT

 You're sensitive and shy and don't project your real self to the world. You feel you have to put on an act to please others.

7AM – 8.59AM ★ DRAGON

 Independent and interesting, you present a picture of someone who is quite out of the ordinary.

9AM – 10.59AM ★ SNAKE

 You can be a bit difficult to fathom and, because you appear so controlled, people either take to you instantly, or not at all.

11AM – 12.59PM ★ HORSE

 Open, cheerful and happy-go-lucky is the picture you always put across to others. You're an extrovert and it generally shows.

1PM – 2.59PM ★ SHEEP

 Your unassuming nature won't allow you to foist yourself upon others so people see you as quiet and retiring – but eminently sensible, though.

3PM – 4.59PM ★ MONKEY

 Lively and talkative, that twinkle in your eye will guarantee you make friends wherever you go.

5PM – 6.59PM ★ ROOSTER

 There's something rather stylish in your approach that gives people an impression of elegance and glamour. But you don't suffer fools gladly.

7PM – 8.59PM ★ DOG

 Some people see you as steady and reliable, others as quiet and graceful and others still as dull and unimaginative. It all depends who you're with at the time.

9PM – 10.59PM ★ PIG

 Your laid-back manner conceals a depth of interest and intelligence that doesn't always come through at first glance.

19

Your hour of birth describes your outer temperament.

*Dragons are
courageous
and blow
away all
fear.*

The Dragon Lover

*For you, relating to
people is easy-peasy.
With such a magnetic
personality you have no
trouble attracting
potential suitors.
Sensual, sassy and highly
sexed, your heart rules
your head.*

LET'S DEAL WITH YOUR NEGATIVE characteristics first – you're tough enough, you can take it. Besides, you respect people who are up-front and stand up to you. For a start, you're a consummate egotist. You're a show-off and love the limelight; modesty is not one of your assets. Then there's your temper, which is the worst of all the Chinese Animals. You can be dogmatic, domineering and bombastic. You hate taking advice from anyone, are quick to rebuke your nearest and dearest and can be hopelessly tactless and insensitive to your partner.

LOVABLE DRAGONS

Why do people love you so much? Because you're warm and generous. You're charismatic and irresistibly attractive and so strong and courageous that standing beside you drives away fear. Your irrepressible exuberance makes the sun shine on the bleakest day and you generate excitement wherever you go. You're wild and impulsive and can make anyone realize their dreams. People love you because, when you're around, everyone simply feels better.

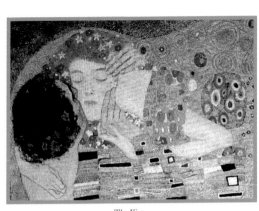

The Kiss
GUSTAV KLIMT 1862–1918

TYING THE KNOT

Though you fall in love at the drop of a hat, you're in no hurry to give up your independence, indeed many Dragons remain confirmed singletons. But an intelligent, witty and amusing companion may well intrigue you enough to make you want to tie the knot. And once Dragon folk become committed they are unlikely to ever roam again.

Once you find the right partner, you remain committed.

In Your Element

ALTHOUGH YOUR SIGN recurs every 12 years, each generation is slightly modified by one of 5 elements. If you were born under the Metal influence your character, emotions and behaviour would show significant variations from an individual born under one of the other elements. Check the Year Chart for your ruling element and discover what effects it has upon you.

THE METAL DRAGON ★ 1940 AND 2000

Honest but intolerant, gutsy but inflexible, you succeed by sheer grit and defiance. You're tough and respect those who can stand up to you; weaker mortals get short shrift. You're a powerful ally in times of trouble but a ferocious opponent to your enemies.

THE WATER DRAGON ★ 1952

Because you're not as impatient and haven't the same burning desire to be the focus of attention as other Dragons, you can stand back and take an objective view. Thus you make wise judgements and are prepared to see eye-to-eye with others.

龍

23

THE WOOD DRAGON ★ 1904 AND 1964

Inquisitive and open-minded, you enjoy discussing new ideas and are receptive to other people's points of view. You're creative and appreciate Art in all its forms. Less egotistical than most Dragons, you're able to build a successful and contented life for yourself.

THE FIRE DRAGON ★ 1916 AND 1976

Wow, what a powerful dynamo you can be! Able to accelerate from cool to explosive in under 60 seconds, you're a force to be reckoned with. If you could manage to control your temper and your passions, or cool that ardour and competitive spirit, you'd find relationships a good deal easier to cope with.

THE EARTH DRAGON ★ 1928 AND 1988

Logical and level-headed, you have a flair for organization and make an excellent manager. At work you're sociable, approachable and co-operative and, compared to other Dragons, less inclined to breathe fire or to erupt like a volcano at the least provocation. In love, you take your responsibilities seriously.

*Rencontre
du Soir
(detail)*
THEOPHILE-
ALEXANDRE
STEINLEN
1859–1923

Partners in Love

THE CHINESE are very definite about which animals are compatible with each other and which are antagonistic. So find out if you're truly suited to your partner.

DRAGON + RAT
★ *A brilliant relationship – plenty of passion, mental rapport and understanding. Star-tipped for happiness and success.*

DRAGON + OX
★ *When it comes to stubbornness, you've met your match here. Where's the give-and-take essential for a happy marriage?*

DRAGON + TIGER
★ *A gutsy combination with plenty of sparks to fuel the passions and the fire.*

Eiaha chipa
PAUL GAUGUIN 1848–1903

DRAGON + RABBIT
★ *Your differences will either unite or divide you.*

DRAGON + DRAGON
★ *If you learn to share the limelight, the world will be your oyster.*

DRAGON + SNAKE
★ *Clever and crafty, flirty and shirty – you fit together like two pieces of a jigsaw puzzle.*

DRAGON + HORSE
★ *A powerful chemistry bonds you two sexually. Reach mind-touch and you'll have one heck of a partnership!*

DRAGON + SHEEP
★ *Despite the sexual attraction, in the long run you're not suited.*

DRAGON + MONKEY
★ *You think alike and understand each other – a combination destined to be happy and successful.*

25

LOVE PARTNERS AT A GLANCE

Dragon with:	Tips on Togetherness	Compatibility
Rat	on cloud nine	♥♥♥♥
Ox	first attraction, then deadlock	♥
Tiger	a dynamic duo!	♥♥♥
Rabbit	learn to give and take	♥♥
Dragon	depends – either heaven or hell	♥♥
Snake	mirror images	♥♥♥
Horse	great sex	♥♥♥
Sheep	different destinies	♥♥
Monkey	refreshingly alive	♥♥♥♥
Rooster	never a dull moment	♥♥
Dog	keep walking if you want to stay healthy	♥
Pig	sooooo comfy	♥♥♥

COMPATIBILITY RATINGS:
♥ *conflict*   ♥♥ *work at it*   ♥♥♥ *strong sexual attraction*   ♥♥♥♥ *heavenly!*

DRAGON + ROOSTER

★ *You're both exquisite creatures and make a gorgeous pair, but your mega-egos tend to get in the way.*

DRAGON + DOG

★ *A truly tempestuous affair that's not recommended for peace of mind.*

DRAGON + PIG

★ *A caring, sharing and deeply loving partnership.*

Some relationships promise an irresistible magnetism.

Christobel Finds Geraldine (detail)
WILLIAM
GERSHAM
COLLINGWOOD
1854–1932

Hot Dates

IF YOU'RE DATING someone for the first time, taking your partner out for a special occasion or simply wanting to re-ignite that flame of passion between you, it helps to understand what would please that person most.

RATS ★ *Wine and dine him or take her to a party. Do something on impulse… go to the races or take a flight in a hot air balloon.*

OXEN ★ *Go for a drive in the country and drop in on a stately home. Visit an art gallery or antique shops. Then have an intimate dinner à deux.*

'So glad to see you…'
COCA-COLA 1945

TIGERS ★ *Tigers thrive on excitement so go clay-pigeon shooting, Formula One racing or challenge each other to a Quasar dual. A date at the theatre will put stars in your Tiger's eyes.*

RABBITS ★ *Gentle and creative, your Rabbit date will enjoy an evening at home with some take-away food and a romantic video. Play some seductive jazz and snuggle up.*

DRAGONS ★ *Mystery and magic will thrill your Dragon date. Take in a son et lumière show or go to a carnival. Or drive to the coast and sink your toes in the sand as the sun sets.*

SNAKES ★ *Don't do anything too active – these creatures like to take life sloooowly. Hire a row-boat for a long, lazy ride down the river. Give a soothing massage, then glide into a sensual jacuzzi together.*

The Carnival
DOIN. GASTON 19/20TH CENTURY

HORSES ★ *Your zany Horse gets easily bored. Take her on a mind-spinning tour of the local attractions. Surprise him with tickets to a musical show. Whatever you do, keep them guessing.*

SHEEP ★ *These folk adore the Arts so visit a museum, gallery or poetry recital. Go to a concert, the ballet, or the opera.*

MONKEYS ★ *The fantastical appeals to this partner, so go to a fancy-dress party or a masked ball, a laser light show or a sci-fi movie.*

ROOSTERS ★ *Grand gestures will impress your Rooster. Escort her to a film première or him to a formal engagement. Dressing up will place this date in seventh heaven.*

DOGS ★ *A cosy dinner will please this most unassuming of partners more than any social occasion. Chatting and story telling will ensure a close understanding.*

PIGS ★ *Arrange a slap-up meal or a lively party, or cruise through the shopping mall. Shopping is one of this partner's favourite hobbies!*

Detail from
Chinese
Marriage
Ceremony
CHINESE
PAINTING

Year of Commitment

CAN THE YEAR in which you marry (or make a firm commitment to live together) have any influence upon your marital relationship or the life you and your partner forge together? According to the Orientals, it certainly can. Whether your marriage is fiery, gentle, productive, passionate, insular or sociable doesn't so much depend on your animal nature, as on the nature of the Animal in whose year you tied the knot.

IF YOU MARRY IN A YEAR OF THE...

RAT ★ *your marriage should succeed because ventures starting now attract long-term success. Materially, you won't want and life is full of friendship.*

Marriage Feast
CHINESE PAINTING

OX ★ *your relationship will be solid and tastes conventional. Diligence will be recognized and you'll be well respected.*

TIGER ★ *you'll need plenty of humour to ride out the storms. Marrying in the Year of the Tiger is not auspicious.*

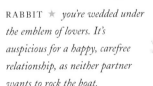

RABBIT ★ *you're wedded under the emblem of lovers. It's auspicious for a happy, carefree relationship, as neither partner wants to rock the boat.*

DRAGON ★ *you're blessed. This year is highly auspicious for luck, happiness and success.*

SNAKE ★ *it's good for romance but sexual entanglements are rife. Your relationship may seem languid, but passions run deep.*

HORSE ★ *chances are you decided to marry on the spur of the moment as the Horse year encourages impetuous behaviour. Marriage now may be volatile.*

SHEEP ★ *your family and home are blessed but watch domestic spending. Money is very easily frittered away.*

Marriage Ceremony
CHINESE PAINTING

MONKEY ★ *married life could be unconventional. As plans go awry your lives could be full of surprises.*

ROOSTER ★ *drama characterizes your married life. Your household will run like clockwork, but bickering could strain your relationship.*

DOG ★ *it's a truly fortunate year and you can expect domestic joy. Prepare for a large family as the Dog is the sign of fertility!*

PIG ★ *it's highly auspicious and there'll be plenty of fun. Watch out for indulgence and excess.*

Marriage Ceremony (detail)
CHINESE PAINTING

Detail from Chinese Marriage Ceremony
CHINESE PAINTING

龍

TYPICAL DRAGON PLEASURES

COLOUR PREFERENCES ★ *Greeny-blue*

Amber

Sapphire

GEMS AND STONES ★ *Opal, sapphire, amber*

SUITABLE GIFTS ★ *Pack of Tarot cards, camera, executive toy, a copy of the I Ching, mirror, a family crest, mobile phone, a reflexology session*

HOBBIES AND PASTIMES ★ *show jumping, computer programming, tennis, public speaking, fossil hunting, amateur dramatics, astrology*

HOLIDAY PREFERENCES ★ *Take a winter break and go skiing, in the summer abseil, parascend or hang-glide. Visit the Wonders of the World and marvel at man's ingenuity. Because you're sentimental, why not retrace your childhood, your undergraduate days or have your honeymoon all over again.*

Iguazu falls on Iguazu river
BRAZILIAN BORDER

COUNTRIES LINKED WITH THE DRAGON ★ *Nepal, Spain, Kenya, Cuba, countries in Latin America*

The Dragon Parent

YOU DRAGON FOLK are so busy climbing the ladder of success, making a name for yourselves, or accumulating wealth that you tend to leave having children until later than most people. Parenting doesn't come naturally or easily to you but, when it does, you approach starting a family with as much gusto as you do everything else. You're as proud of your offspring as of your other achievements – and you're never backwards in letting people know about your little ones' talents and their good looks.

31

Once Dragons decide to have children they make proud parents.

PROTECTION

You take parental responsibilities seriously. You're kind but firm, ambitious for your offspring and protective of their welfare. Should any problem upset them, or mishap befall them, you will brandish your metaphorical sword and, in typical avenging-angel style, immediately set off to redress all wrongs.

THE DRAGON HABITAT

You're not really a domestic creature at all and are happier out in the world. But you are creative with an appreciation of aesthetics and, because you're flamboyant, it's unlikely that you'll live in a dingy, poky hovel. Your home has to be big and imposing to match your personality, sumptuous to accommodate your sensuality and opulent enough to reflect your prestige.

Animal Babies

FOR SOME parents, their children's personalities harmonize perfectly with their own. Others find that no matter how much they may love their offspring they're just not on the same wavelength. Our children arrive with their characters already well formed and, according to Chinese philosophy, shaped by the influence of their Animal Year. So you should be mindful of the year in which you conceive.

BABIES BORN IN THE YEAR OF THE...

RAT ★ *love being cuddled. They keep on the go – so give them plenty of rest. Later they enjoy collecting things.*

OX ★ *are placid, solid and independent. If not left to their own devices they sulk.*

TIGER ★ *are happy and endearing. As children, they have irrepressible energy. Boys are sporty and girls tom-boys.*

RABBIT ★ *are sensitive and strongly bonded to their mother. They need stability to thrive.*

DRAGON ★ *are independent and imaginative from the start. Encourage any interest that will allow their talents to flourish.*

SNAKE ★ *have great charm. They are slow starters so may need help with school work. Teach them to express feelings.*

龍

33

One Hundred Children Scroll
ANON, MING PERIOD

HORSE ★ *will burble away contentedly for hours. Talking starts early and they excel in languages.*

SHEEP ★ *are placid, well-behaved and respectful. They are family-oriented and never stray too far from home.*

MONKEY ★ *take an insatiable interest in everything. With agile minds they're quick to learn. They're good-humoured but mischievous!*

ROOSTER ★ *are sociable. Bright and vivacious, their strong adventurous streak best shows itself on a sports field.*

DOG ★ *are cute and cuddly. Easily pleased, they are content just pottering around the house amusing themselves for hours. Common sense is their greatest virtue.*

PIG ★ *are affectionate and friendly. Well-balanced, self-confident children, they're happy-go-lucky and laid-back. They are popular with friends.*

*With your
adaptability
and fresh
approach you
are suited
to any
occupation.*

Health, Wealth and Worldly Affairs

DESPITE THE FACT that you run on high octane energy, burn the candle at both ends and take breathtaking risks, you are blessed with good health. You belong to one of the more robust Animal signs and any ill-health you might suffer is likely to be caused by stress. Tension headaches are common amongst Dragons, and emotional storms may contribute to depression or hypertension. Getting some routine into your life or practising Yoga should help.

CAREER

You're never afraid of taking a risk, so going off at a tangent invariably proves successful and highly lucrative to boot.

Of the many talents you bring to your work it's your originality that stands out. Whatever your field (and being adaptable means you're suited to any occupation), you always take a fresh and radical approach. Not only distinctly creative, you're also a genius at lateral thinking; you can see new avenues where others see only brick walls.

35

FINANCES

On the negative side, you're a big spender. You're prone to taking whopping big risks with your capital, and sometimes you'll bet your shirt and lose it. On the positive side, you're honest as the live-long day, never cheat and were born with the Midas touch, so no self-respecting Dragon remains penniless for long.

Dragons are ambitious and status-conscious. Naturally bossy, you have to be in charge and be the biggest fish in the biggest pond. Whether it is because you're a workaholic or because you have the most colossal cheek, it doesn't take you long to reach the top.

Dragons are ambitious and so many are workaholics.

FRIENDSHIPS

With your tempestuous, fiery nature you're not the most comfortable friend for anyone who is sensitive or timorous. But those who know and love you find you kind and benevolent, a true champion and a terrific ally in times of trouble. Never a fair-weather friend, once you have pledged your allegiance you will never let that person down – a friend is a friend for life.

DRAGONS MAKE EXCELLENT:

Computer analysts ★ Inventors ★ Engineers ★ Architects
Lawyers ★ Philosophers ★ Psychoanalysts ★ Brokers
Managers ★ Sales personnel ★ PR people ★ Advertising agents
Officers in the armed forces ★ Campaigners ★ Politicians

36

East Meets West

COMBINE YOUR Oriental Animal sign with your Western Zodiac birth sign to form a deeper and richer understanding of your character and personality.

ARIES DRAGON

★ With your drive and enthusiasm, you cram as much as you can into your day, never letting anything or anyone stand in the way of what you want. You're in love with love.

TAUREAN DRAGON

★ Taurus brings you down to earth. Material comforts are essential to you as are love and security. Highly sexed, with the right partner you are faithful for life.

GEMINI DRAGON

★ If talking and flirting were Olympic sports, you'd get two gold medals. You're one of life's performers, at your best when centre-stage. But you're warm, generous and interested in people.

CANCERIAN DRAGON

★ Artistically gifted, you have refined tastes. Your home reflects this and is a show-case for your talents. Caring and sensitive, a close relationship and settled home are essential to your happiness.

LEONINE DRAGON

★ The luckiest and most charismatic of the Dragons, your warmth and joie de vivre make you irresistibly attractive. In love matters you aim high.

VIRGO DRAGON

★ Status matters to you and you'll work hard to reach the standard of living you desire. Your work and social life are carefully planned. You're likely to put off starting a family until later.

LIBRAN DRAGON

★ Libran's aesthetic sense added to the Dragon élan makes you a stylish creature. Your charm is your greatest asset and draws people to you. In love you can be irresponsible so a partner who is practical makes an ideal mate.

SCORPIO DRAGON

★ A powerful personality with intense emotions and a strong sex drive, your compelling, hypnotic quality attracts potential partners like bees to a honey-pot. When you love, you love obsessively and expect your partner to reciprocate.

SAGITTARIAN DRAGON

★ Your forthright honesty, though well intentioned, can be insensitive so a little more diplomacy wouldn't go amiss. Your sunshiny personality and exuberant gusto for life sweep everything before you. Your life is a broad and colourful canvas.

CAPRICORN DRAGON

★ Love and romance all too often take second place to your career. You're compelled to climb the ladder of success and may put your personal life on hold in favour of your worldly aspirations, but once committed, you're responsible and dutiful.

AQUARIAN DRAGON

★ Idealistic and unconventional, you're perhaps the most unorthodox of the Dragons. You're an intellectual first and foremost, and an individualist. Broad-minded, you're tolerant of the vagaries of life and the sexual predilections of others.

PISCEAN DRAGON

★ All Pisceans have drop-dead good looks. You're an intriguing mixture of sensitivity and strength of will; you appear placid but underneath, your feelings are all astir. This can make it difficult for you to know what you truly want in a relationship.

FAMOUS DRAGONS

Martin Luther King

John Lennon

Salvador Dali

Princess Stephanie

Florence Nightingale

Jeffrey Archer ★ *Yehudi Menuhin*
Zandra Rhodes ★ *Placido Domingo*
Jenny Agutter ★ *Joan Baez* ★ *Al Pacino*
Prince Edward ★ *Eartha Kitt*
Richard Pryor ★ *James Garner*
Frank Zappa ★ *Lewis Carroll*
Friedrich Nietzsche ★ *John Lennon*
Salvador Dali ★ *Bing Crosby*
Martin Luther King
Abraham Lincoln ★ *Ringo Starr*
Charles Darwin ★ *Oscar Wilde*

Bing Crosby

The Dragon Year in Focus

DRAMA CHARACTERIZES the Dragon Year both in lavish events and unpredictability. The year is marked at its beginning and end by significant international developments. The bizarre and the unexpected are associated with the razzmatazz of this sign.

THE ARTS

The performing Arts, fashion and cultural events come under favourable auspices, the more original, the better. Magnificent projects and outlandish schemes are the order of the day. The feel-good factor will sweep us along on a wave of elation; risks will be taken, fortunes made and lost.

The Dragon Year is particularly auspicious for artistic ventures.

GOOD FORTUNE

As the Dragon brings good fortune, this is an auspicious year in which to get married and to have a baby, since Dragon children bring luck to the household. Starting a business or initiating a major project now will all bring success.

ACTIVITIES ASSOCIATED
WITH THE DRAGON YEAR

The invention, inauguration, patenting or first use of:
the thermos flask, FIFA, stainless steel cutlery, scheduled television service, electron microscope, Civil Rights movement, mechanical heart, genetically altered mouse.

40

Your Dragon Fortunes
for the Next 12 Years

1996 MARKS THE BEGINNING of a new 12-year cycle in the Chinese calendar. How your relationships and worldly prospects fare will depend on the influence of each Animal year in turn.

1996 YEAR OF THE RAT   *19 Feb 1996 – 6 Feb 1997*

Dragons are at their best when the pace is lively and exciting and 1996 promises to be just that. Corner the market with your lateral thinking and come up with something new that will capture the spirit of the moment. The course of love runs smooth.

YEAR TREND: SHOW YOUR METTLE

1997 YEAR OF THE OX   *7 Feb 1997 – 27 Jan 1998*

Let probity be your watchword in business and in your romantic life – particularly for singletons embarking on a new love affair. Success comes to those who keep their heads down and progress steadily. Heart's ease is found amongst established relationships.

YEAR TREND: SLOW BUT SURE

1998 YEAR OF THE TIGER   *28 Jan 1998 – 15 Feb 1999*

Relationships may not be all they appear on the surface this year, so beware all you Dragons who dislike any form of commitment. This applies just as much to romantic ties as to business associates.

YEAR TREND: YOU CAN'T PLEASE EVERYBODY

1999 YEAR OF THE RABBIT · *16 Feb 1999 – 4 Feb 2000*

Expect a calmer year – a good time to reap the fruits of past endeavours. Wise Dragons will gather their energies for the galvanic events of 2000, which kick-start the new millennium.

YEAR TREND: A TIME FOR RECUPERATION

2000 YEAR OF THE DRAGON · *5 Feb 2000 – 23 Jan 2001*

The frenetic beat that accompanies your own year will come as music to your ears. Your efforts will be recognized and rewarded and success will follow. Romantic interludes quicken your pulse.

YEAR TREND: LOVE IS HIGH ON THE AGENDA

The Year of the Snake proves very profitable as your chickens come home to roost.

2001 YEAR OF THE SNAKE · *24 Jan 2001 – 11 Feb 2002*

Friends and associates will hear you say, 'I told you so!' repeatedly this year and watch you rub your hands with glee as your chickens come home to roost. You can rake in the profits of past endeavours, but lovers feel ignored.

YEAR TREND: SHOW LOVED ONES YOU CARE

12 YEARS
OF DRAGON
FORTUNES

龍

41

42

2002 YEAR OF THE HORSE *12 Feb 2002 – 31 Jan 2003*

There's an unpredictable quality about this year but you like thinking on your feet and are adaptable enough to capitalize handsomely on its vagaries. Your diary will be full and your love life turns on the heat.

YEAR TREND: IT'S PARTY TIME!

2003 YEAR OF THE SHEEP *1 Feb 2003 – 21 Jan 2004*

Although you prefer a livelier pace, after the relentless onslaught of the Horse Year, 2003 will come as a relief and give you time to draw breath; take every opportunity to rest and recuperate. For those who can get away, romance beckons in distant climes.

YEAR TREND: A YEAR FOR TYING UP LOOSE ENDS

2004 YEAR OF THE MONKEY *22 Jan 2004 – 8 Feb 2005*

Events happen thick and fast this year and many opportunities come your way. However, don't chance too much to luck, or overstretch your resources. A bit of give and take on your part will help to smooth relationships and keep partners sweet.

YEAR TREND: PUT LOVED ONES FIRST

The Year of the Rooster means advancement in your power and status.

2005 YEAR OF THE ROOSTER 9 Feb 2005 – 28 Jan 2006

In Rooster years you make meteoric advances in your life. Whether it's fame and fortune, position and power, status and prestige or love and romance that you seek, with Lady Luck positively smiling on you throughout 2005, how can you fail to succeed?

YEAR TREND: A TIME FOR SUPERLATIVE ACHIEVEMENT

2006 YEAR OF THE DOG *29 Jan 2006 – 17 Feb 2007*

A tricky year when you must practise patience and learn to count to ten before you speak. Any hitches and setbacks at work are more than offset by a settled and contented home life.

YEAR TREND: KEEP A LOW PROFILE

2007 YEAR OF THE PIG *18 Feb 2007 – 6 Feb 2008*

A highly productive and progressive year in which you can make up any ground lost last year. Chances are you could come into some money. Socially, the scene is exciting with plenty of invitations and parties; if single, you could meet the partner of your destiny now.

YEAR TREND: THE UNEXPECTED COMES UP TRUMPS